W9-BWI-320

Volume 64 of the
Yale Series of Younger Poets
edited by Dudley Fitts
and published with aid from
the Mary Cady Tew Memorial Fund

URANIUM POEMS

by Judith Johnson Sherwin

New Haven and London
Yale University Press
1969

Library of Congress catalog card number: 69–15460
Designed by Marvin Howard Simmons,
set in Times Roman type,
and printed in the United States of America by
the Carl Purington Rollins Printing-Office of the
Yale University Press, New Haven, Connecticut.
Distributed in Great Britain, Europe, Asia, and
Africa by Yale University Press Ltd., London; in
Canada by McGill University Press, Montreal; and
in Latin America by Centro Interamericano de Libros
Académicos, Mexico City.
Acknowledgment is made to the following
publications for poems which originally appeared
in them: *Beloit Poetry Journal, Literary Review, New
England Review, Poetry Northwest, Southwest Review*.
The poem "Watersong" was first published in *Poetry*.

PUBLISHER'S PREFACE

Judith Johnson Sherwin was the last of the nine Yale Younger Poets selected by Dudley Fitts after he became Editor of the Series in 1959. Unfortunately, he was unable to prepare one of his typically cogent introductions to her work, although in a letter written just before his untimely death in June 1968 he characterized it as "exciting—unconventional, staccato, colloquial, full of wit."

Deprived of Fitts' editing, Mrs. Sherwin sought advice from one of his earliest choices, Alan Dugan. He liked her poems and was helpful. Later he wrote to Yale:

> *Uranium Poems* is not just another moral polemic about nuclear energy and the culture that produced it. Mrs. Sherwin's poems have a vigorous, solid, unsentimental musicality about them which goes beyond moral indignation. Let me stress the word "musicality" and be clear about it. The poems are not imitations of music. They are associated, as words, with music.

Everyone connected with the Yale Younger Poets program will miss Dudley Fitts. This volume, we believe, attests once again the catholic taste and lively judgment which made him such a valued adviser to the Yale University Press and an acceptable mentor to nine fine poets.

to Whom it may concern

Lord in the matter of your ninety-second element
(rare, heavy, greyish, found especially in pitchblende and
uranite
eager for evil, made for misrule)
let me most earnestly advise you:

alter the weight, let the nucleus be
lighter or heavier, as you please to imagine,
but cohesive, resistant to bombardment
and the shocks metal inherits;

let the substance be black or blue
or scarlet as sin, that we may know what we do;

let it be common as dirt, that all may use
it as they choose,
the head of state
and the atomized states of individual hunger
who are his body politic;

or let it be found filigreed, entwined in veins
of marble in art's most valued monuments,
that we may fear to scratch it out
lest we crack the image of civilization;

this element, if it be apt to evil, educate
it to elude us, not cooperate
when we break it to our desire.
redeem it, stand in fire
at Hiroshima or blister under the skin
with your fishermen in the pacific sea
when the element is tried and found wanting
or not wanting

as waywardly it may seem to be:
wanting: in its very breaking to be
your death, mine, transubstantiate you or me;
not wanting: that what was should be
your universe unchanged, the element
fixed in its rank, obedient
as a star to do your will.

if it is still
incorrigible
after your sacrifice by blister
your radiation of passion,
after the very seed and day
in you of all our years turn mutant,
cast it into the fires of greatest heat
that it may meet
the hurt it brings you and your fishermen
this dawnless day
enduring still Hiroshima, here.
let it be broken in hell, let the fires there
burn out each other, let that heat fuse to silence
in the ice-clear sight of unchanged charity.
now, while you may,
let this element die
in us; mine
it from our minds,
delve
it out of ourselves
where it lies rare, heavy, greyish, in pitchblende
of our desires.
let man your self-reflecting universe
be made without uranium.

Lord, while you may, i earnestly advise
you, lift this destructive element from your mind, excise
it, let it be
in the void, unmade, unnamed, unthought, let this be
our dream of salvation.

CONTENTS

Part One:

A SWEET GOODNIGHT

the prospector's complaint

HAPPY JACK'S ROCK

mine, better tell no man
    what a don't care deep down rock ribbed stubborn
        what a cold fish tight fisted underhanded punch
        drunk son of a butter fingered bitch you were
            let it all go for him
            wouldn't let me in

better tell no man
    you spit-tinkled me out like a beer drinking river
    slag wash down the mountainside
    of the twenty lives i dug for you

happy jack mine
better tell no man
    how you rolled right over on your rockbottom flapjack
    buttered side for those memo-dripping stickpin
    eyes in a two button suit with computer ears
        and a twenty-four carat ruby red ringtailed ass
                                                            and a tennis
            playing pool swimming soft corporation
            attached you could drown in and never even know it

better tell no man
    in your fat cat song purring sharpy rocktoothed
    mouth what a river pissing goldfishing underground
        played out dug up   gold gone bad
        ore washed up   copper mined out   silver snaggle
                                                                    teeth
            pulled out assets frozen act you put on
                for me and then came
                for his kitchen magic

                                        and the drowning A-frame
houses and the fireball dustcloud burnt up world
rocking down to the toothroot shaken bones
of the flick built villages sang
    out don't hand it over don't hand
    it over baby earthworm grub-hatching rainbow grit boweled
    man-eating harbor of all of us don't
        lay it all down right on the dotted line
        high-priced spread
            out wide open for him
        in a beautiful milkwhite porcelain polished
            industry wide grin
        with a cashbox rattling stock splitting mashed
            potato dancing shiver built in.

happy jack you golden chock full of fucks
bullseye of the golden west
    no one ever tell you better to go
    down dignified
    for no man
    than this worldwide
    twitch of the limbs for death
that shuts us out most when it takes us in?

THE EARTH: TO MARILYN

hey brassy baby whose switched-on hair
made them glow in the dark
call for a brand new smile to wear
in the long nights when the geiger counters
praise you, when dream goal
of a thousand quick-buck loud tuft hunters
you go down measured / call
for a trickier hip swivel
to flick the slow worm fingers off, drop out
the ball from the socket, the joint
from its fleshbound background, tune
the strings away

from their fixed tonality / call
a halt to that plumed tale
of wealth they caught fluttering out of your walk
(made needles rise, that crazy click
go-go: we've struck the mother-lode) / call for
a girdle of stainless steel
fitted with three padlocks, seven sharp spikes to stick
whatever plunders you   /   for a quick
mind feel.

lady of spending in dreams when i see
under your put-on costumes of intellect
how rich
delicious you were made
madonna of money, my promised score
when the sound tracks
out when the blind hair screen
screams black and nothing's
paying i detest the waste
of life, loin's hurry, mind's fast

that came to this long feast
for you and me
now we two are filled
your mouth with me
mine with you

SUITE FOR DANCE BAND

I

see where the night shakes, tuning
one silver ping on the fork of Berenice's Hair
the very first a
in me / see where
the bones dance play,
the snake my fellow
an air going wish wish
in the folded accordion whose playing's my heart,
knockjangle knuckles folding
unfolding its rhythm / my old dance dress
arms empty, hung up by the black silk holes in its elbows
wrists limp, hiss-whispers how swish is Death

II

what else should i wish wish
see he is
smooth. taffeta leaves he moves
through woodwind ear channels / makes lips push
the sound out / saving
his breath, is more than breath /
strung tight: on strings, between strings weaves
the cold night hair
into no holding
back, his rest no rest / loops brass
coiled springs in the full skull
and the barrel loins where you push push
your waves breaking my stops

III

on that night in the future that will not pass
see where
the snake my fellow
was every air going
wish in the folded rhythm of shuttles weaving
the black silk accordion plays my heart /
was where the hollow
bell bones knuckled under, rung
in a bending unbending cardboard spine-strung-
through-the-back-of-the-neck-on-down
rag flapping / all nights our bones played shady
dance tunes, rang silver-ping a's, struck lazy
moon gongs in our musical animal
were no more than physic and germinal
swelling to break wind out in a burst where
the coiled airs broke apart

LADY ON THE A TRAIN

what sits here leans or is thrown
against her, dances thigh against
thigh, loin smacking loin
exchanging vows, closely assessed may be a germ;
or, if she take the mere lust

of the beast for accomplishment, animal
at best. she is attacked
in her seat by merchants of rhythm, adulterate mixers, the fact
of being moved is the dread fall,
terror of being bought traded sold, must infect

her most static will. she
is attacked by scavengers, parasites, snot
spun out of the delicate nostrils of cleanliness. now while she
counts her stations, sanitary but quick, she
wills to stop, she will not stop, it is not

her stop. the diseases gather to burrow, touch, untruffle
her quite, rooting, rear back their heads, exhale, let sound the
call
her blood comes to, the jack-of-all-will
call, mortal, blood answering offal:
traders, invaders, how shall your music move me and i not fall?

MIKE FINK TO WIN

said the great green gator to mike the river
with a crack in me head late
at night what mastermind mad chessplayer
banged you down on this white square
with your big jaws tied, teeth filed, scaled tail cut
not a live man hand, not a black hambone
but this lean branch to snap at? *mike:*
blood brother:
i've the ragtime night to eat.

said the killer bronc throwback to mike hoss-buster
split through the mitre late
tell me the name of the mean witchdoctor
bogey-man trapped you in this horsehair
this stiff peaked hat, blackface rig, preaching trade
to the half-baked savages, rived the game
from you, put the bones on you, not a bale of hay
but a blackface shine / down river
for you to look at till morning? *mike:*
turf-brother
i've the ragtime night to eat.

totem, pledge of me fathers, make me a squeal
in me cloven skull late
river kingsize, five moves deep to shout how
no wild ditchdigger planted me here
brought back on me bare back rock scalps
tungsten bearmeat, tin beaverpelt
copper rich green brown fur of the land
to melt in me pot / death with a lilt to it
there is no shaman anywhere
alive who could ragtie me teeth, horsehair
me rock-smashed down on this white square brother
with the ragtime night to eat.

BANDIT / VEGAS

when you turned me on
lover my shining dime
in this sandbend town, bells spun chiffon
foam torrents / the measured odds-on favorite rhine
girls purled in the spun gold
river-pledged wealth / lights rang up, spelled,
stood on end, stretched out over my gilded
skull in a tense hair chorus-line /
the rainbow scaled
trout bellied over the rock
falls of a town weighed out
short / each round thin
paring counted, sang
out jackpot / the whole damn machine
turning the wrong trick spat coins out.

when i was a market-wise coin-
catching gadget and you were a country boy turned
city fisher, the more you stuck
in somehow the more you might take
out some day some night
at payoff time when you pulled out
your hands locked
just under the join of my chrome tailfin
your booted foot
stamped my silver payday head on the block
your river-telling knife scraped back
against the grain, worried the slant of me, stripped, flayed,
popped
the thin half-moon
pared scales up, jumping the light-
fall torrents. you took back

with you the wire light-
waving chorus-line scalp
trophy, took
the bells dancing jackpot my wealth spilled
into a drawer marked change.

i couldn't remember to count
lover the shining times
my gold sun lay down
full of the coin
haul you left / some day some night
the more you might take out
under ground i felt cold
the more i might collect
when the odds weigh right
the eyes see what the mind will reject.

HAPPY JACK'S STOMP

named it for me
i nightly swear
in a tapdance hurry

ladies walked
gardens with golden apple
hands that kept the world young

and slapdash boast
eyes awash in beer
i daily double
or nothing say

here
these hairy hands are not ice but bone

got thar too late
to cash chips in
gold silver or copper
iron tin

on the mountain women
's beautiful hairy cheeks
too

soon to dig
in a pussy-foot flutter
238 out
you can hear me holler
clear up the alcan
needle a-fluster

i was a thing
yesterday i was a longbeard thorn
in the flesh of Jiminy Cricket's
split level vision

way into Blind River
way way too late
to get the hell out

IF YOU KNOCK

knock on my door i'm
not buying any not giving any
away not
            the dry rot the wet rot the brown rot on celery stalks
having any today knives
not sharpened broken-strawed brooms stacked
in the closet old clothes piled
            lettuce rot bread rot breast rot head rot
any old how under the bed and the moths
can have them but not you fresh
fruit and vegetables can dream
            (exposed
            on sidewalk counters of the green
            rot inbetween rot fish
            showcased in ice lay bare
            their slivered mirror bellies shine up at me hope)
of being bought
it is the earth
in me makes me cry
hoarse strident objectionable the cars on her
impersonal ornaments strung round my throat
pass me by

PROJECTIONS

yes you said but
take that slot machine
did it really feel
cheated when
it came
wasn't that what
it was made for
was that
maybe you
saying yourself through
it

don't you believe
things have voices that
speak (to you speak
human voices

not
their own voices we put
in them)

but
voices put
in them are their own
saying what you say you
make it so
you
make it yours

saying them through

themselves you make them say

what they are

(would be if they could

say it

poor old slot

machine taken for what)

she's not

bang baby had

real bad

just can't leave her alone
there she is / made

again

WATERSONG

under your fishwiggle thrust
in channel and lock to feel
    skin whispers to skin
the gold seed spill
tally of days and all
holding back a forgotten taste

in salmonleaping in-
lets scale ringing scale to hear
    skin whispers to skin
hammer the grain sheer
hands, in the still pools' measure
to see fin hairy on fin

brush, winesweat and ripe to smell
the thick fur weeds leaf loose
    skin whispers to skin
the soul from their black juice-
steeped roots, and song bruise
stagger the stone-lipped well,

goldslithering, rustle a brew
out of the still place
    skin whispers to skin
that is lost yes in your face
to touch what is not you

NIGHTPIECE

not to touch, she said to me, anything sticky
oil hairgoo pitgooch rancid facecream spoilt
vegetables, overripe and stepped down around
the dried crud at the curb, shaking flaked soot from her hair
any kind of filth that could rub off on me, not
to feel, she begged me, wash swallow and swirl of just any
old slime sloshing, and the little white scaly seeds
scattered the riding winds of a city's dandruff
not to break down inside me, she promised, the barrier
that keeps what i use from touching what i am, and took
one giant step over the rainbow rings on the black
skin of an oil pool, not not not to absorb
in my veins the jackhammer jolt
of what i despise, and tripped delicately past
the red splat of pizza, waded the tiny pink
bobbing faces trapped in the vomit marsh
on the IND stairs, raking
her dress from her thighs with the fingers of their smell,
walked through the glass showcase
stares of queers in the mirror doors *sweetheart when you sat*
at the mirror i saw that longhair greaseball Death
with hands toothed as plows, harrow
right through the ticketed marked-down sale
merchandise that would have raped her if she had looked
one come-on *and jerking his head, with an ingratiating smile*
comb
the meat from your bones in strings and right on through
all the people that might rub off, the blood lymph mucous that
bubbles
over the line between it and you inside you, doesn't know when
to stop *pretty*
you up for the night, carding
your wool with his knotted fingers

GRANDPA JOHNSON AND BLIND RIVER BLUES

takes a couple of minutes but it feels like more
should when you go with it . . .
    he had a cane
    with a gold head   gold watch chain
    was a moose or an elk or what grazes here
    banged down the door with his bighand horns
    left his wife his mortgage and his teenage son
    dad wrote i was born   no word
    could be living now for all i know
    one of the longtooth mean undead

in omaha long hair
a beard you could pan gold in
a quick hip jiggle and a big black hat
his eyepatch could dance the floor down
    no word and the music loud
    in his mind where he was shaking
    the rockies up and the redwoods down

to fairbanks kicking the old alcan
    late and his eyes / blue teeth in his palms
    where the fingers grew nostrils / snuffed gelt in
    with a goldhead cane   alderman's blues
    elkhead shaking the gold fleas loose

hoofing it down
    the horns spread wide and each horn hand
    selling tickets to the promised
    no word so

didn't touch hands   didn't touch feet
elbows shook out feathers   knees kept beat
bellies slapped out a mirror game

after everyone came   felt just the same
blind river   don't stop here
what to take when i leave: what a gold
        head slid through to dowse out rivers
        underblind
        shaking it out with an open hand
                                                            in a muddy gully
        with any kind of meat and a two fin belly
        shark eye teeth and a mantan suit
        a big sound in the crystal set

of the elkhorns and one   way to go   in
one   way to go   out   no word
don't know / where they went
left me   bitter   lent
carnival ai carnival
don't stop here
blind river carry me away
        where i take out his eyes for a diamond ring
        his teeth for a rock handful plant come spring
        big elkhead nailed to my door
        a rich vein of his blood piped
        to burn in the furnace when the nights chill
        milk of money spurt from his cock
        buy a new grandpa shake out a new night
        when the elkhorns wilt and the child dropped

in the blind river   no word more
couple of minutes   felt like more

CONSTRUCTION ♯ 13

Eichmann before his death
testing wires knots in his mind might have said:
tell me whose death it was
that was contrived at the line's end
where the gaily painted station
pulled in for the night
the trompe d'oeil lives stretched
net vistas of fields trees walks
where none were: if it was theirs
for whom it has been claimed if
there were tears i never tasted
them if there was blood i
never tested it
if it was mine
who constructed with welder's torch
and timetable pliers that neat mesh
of tensions divided the spaces balanced
the shapes made abstract art
of the possible, where was the will
in suspension
in a tension
of fluids?

sun and moon
he named them but they give
no heat no light
metal structures, no more:
light runs on not from them.
death
is an artifact like any other.

you might say
what was needed was to have known
then, while it was running out, what
it was: hearts' blood caught
in the veins' net, or a balance
of salts.   let the analyst test
solutions / potent to make more than paper
change color the catalyst dip
into mystery unchanged   i say
the technique will always outweigh
the purpose.

i might say
sitting pretty within
this wire construction your
body   my deathcage see
me as i was in you
it admitted no final
solution the ambiguity
they called my will.

LIGHTS, FLOWERS

and a sweet goodnight to you
  and you
and a sweet goodnight to you

no sleeping beauty in longhair
  shirt
no sackclad penitent wanes

where the sunlamp sheds its
  violet

no full-bosomed queen of
  sorrows reigns

where the flowering polelamp
  leaps to
the giant's ceiling, drops
  purple and blue

beans down, no courtesan
corset in boredom, long
well-cured nails with the latest
  cut
of mini-i've-seen-it-all put on

in the hum of the winged
  upstairs
lighting fixture sings

i love you, her hourglass dress
  seeping time down
to make your desire stop
just short of the knees, no

flower of the broom
brush my eyes clean

of this room is your wife
but a flat-chested sag-breasted
  slightly hook-nosed not too
razorback

flower of the maize

i won't complain when the
  money

sweep out this corn

flower of délice
slice
me a deep sleep tonight

flower
of the bluet cut
breast and hip to fit

moonlamp only in
its dew please don't

of my days fights back
not rock the bed with any
guilt for the wardead the
dreamstarved
not lament what i've not done

from neckbones to kneecaps /
there is
no better anywhere than this

no madsong
singing maid am i to drown
no hag-
ridden goodwife to cut wrists
when my indirect-lit plastic
hair dome
the carelessness of sleep sheds
touch these bones
they bite

Part Two:

GEOMETRIES

𝄽

THAT SILENCE WAS THE LOVESONG
I WROTE YOU LAST NIGHT WHEN
SHAKING ITS HONKY-TONK TAMBOURINE HAIR
THE NIGHT
SAID TO ME do you need
anybody?
no sweetheart I SAID what
i need if i could find
it maybe a surgically clean mind
and a depopulated city or two
to stretch my belly, laughdance the girders down, tell
what that white space was Blaze
Pascal cloud high, let him shimmy on back to say
how beautiful anarchy broke down
the dancehall let the new years bells fall
the gulls and the alley-cats squall all night
old chrome weeks the corpses of cars pile up
roof high and paper snow
the surplus sardines down with love
lyrics full of get-up-and-go-
somewhere-else-with-your-god-damn-moxie
LIE DOWN REAL SLOW
WITH ME SOME FINE DAY YOU CAN HEAR
THE WORDS PUSH BY:
got more to do with time
than lay around waiting for you
to pick up what that rest you just heard was
all how about i swear
before this year swims out
i'll write you one sweet clean lyric

HAPPY JACK'S HAMMER SONG

bang it out bang it out bang it out damn
bang it damn bang it damn bang baby in the rock
        said Asians
        are Gods came slambang broke
        flint knifeblades to nothing, nerves
        held us to heaven (earth) hammered
        out of us, ore we opened
        only for stone (we were
        stone) outraged, tore for the tough
        stuff they took from it, strip
        mined down

damn bang nothing coming
out today great Thor hard
God of the hammer hammer now
thunder with me / Odin make me see
with two glass eyes what you see with one
        said Aesir
        are / the reason
        in chaos the center the flowery
        kingdom of thought jeweled
        north way to bang it out norway
        south sudden to lick it out sweden
        bang it out from mark out the danes' mark
        forced us from field
        garth and gully of earth in us so
        we died.   Lokiiiiii

jump up jump up jump up the rock
Loki lick it lick it up Loki lick it
up take it take it all if i can't
                                        have it let no man
                                                        brought

metal (and dane
gelded us) gilt
taught us the words and the signs
of the power. we are the first
fell for them this ae nichte
and every nichte and alle we are the frost
giants they called us great stone trolls

slow, clumsy, baresark, caved in the vein
you hammer now hammer now bang
lick it   Loki   last of us
                                        the Rūs
redbrown tundra (hammered out selves
in the star-pierced night steel grit grown into the guilt Mozaic Law
figures in the Temple
Hagia Sophia) baron
of normandy, barone
(south, evil they ferried)
to vineland oversea / powers signs
al jebr of mind made king.

                                                    frost
giants no workers of wonder old stone
in the earth before
the separation mind
hammer mind hammer break it down
break it down (was one) big bang
blow it up big bang to the sky (was low
flowed close to the quick in us) hammer Thor
it out what was   /   ground dirt
under my skin.

why i in my cold
mouth can raise wind
make rain come
say manGods (in the thick furred
tongue of protest) back
bang it down bang it down bang baby in the rock
down hammer your brother
Aesir in Asia build Asgard
and bloody Valhalla there at the rainbow foot
Bifrost of the worldbridge make them hold
open their doors to the signs
and the powers they named / power
on power break where it broke from /   LOUD

and they swore /   we have done . . .

Hoder   Loki   Fenris   Hel

what   shall   protect   this place   when Surt's
fire   burns
                                        heaven and earth

MIKE FINK MY HERO HEE

haw here, not a hoss
but a damnfool mangy-back mule, pointed ears
flick the flies off / here see the meanest cuss
alive by his own boast / take a look, see
the fencepost mane march down the neckridge
(marks off
the neck from the neck oh boundaries
where you don't need 'em
here
no boundary where lucky-buck hooves should clip
the see ya later three-toed forepaws split
brown horsehair on the scaled belly sprouts
alligator flagstone patches down
to the salespitch-lashing tale
mike, let
out a big-boat thoroughbred squawk for the ladies
from your headlong snout, lips curled outward, big
square tooth-pickets all the way back to the cheekbone, straw
stuck between them / what am i bid
for these razzledazz jazzman nostrils flare
(a hole, it has
circumferences, one on, overlapping another, each
one ring that holds in nothing)
if you don't like
to be entered, poked into by my
arriving finger, then just give the gentlemen there
a load of that big-sound spirit, fight back, twitch, blast
trumpet a loud ellis island stay-out, raise the price
on 'em

good ol' mike
stopped at your manifest destiny, finger-stuffed, salted
down too late   spiled
for the last best fight of all
museumed, mounted by housewives small boys teenage girls,
tell all
the folks back home don't knock
that half horse half alligator twofer
one combination price mansize hero
sandwich if yer ready to eat 'im when the winter's hard
rare up, neigh
your rage, let 'em hear each sliced
section whinny or nothing will grow
in you nothing will open up
thick blubbergabble a hole to suck you in / this way, look
no division: NOW
HEAR THIS. HEAR ME SQUEAL
THE RINGTAILED ROARER CAUGHT
IN PRAIRIEMARSHMUDRIVERFLAT-
BOAT TRAFFIC, STOOD UP ON LEGS MUCH
TOO
SOLD SHORT. / NOT MINGO WYANDOTTE
NOT BLACK
SKIN NIGGER NOR ANY WHITE
YANKEE STAY-AT-HOME HORSETRADER
COULD
PUT ME WHERE THIS BOAST
CARRIED ME THIS SWAMP
well take
away your skin containing you tell
me what grows out of you then

E! DURENDAL, CUM ES BEL ET SEINTISME!

just to be rid of it all
let's go down to the sea again clear-eyed
empty dispassionate rid
of the mortal coil
the sea the clean
beach where ignorant armies
unwound downhill fast
strip off the skin you loved so well
with a tweezer's point pick out vein
strings / hang them up to dry
where hands were
what we call
personal / membrane of my sex hung
drips over the bathtub, losing its fit
eyes scooped out shoot
dispassionate stills of the way of a man
with a made in the night we call
dead / rid
of getting up in the morning the answering
service done
once and for all
with love who are you
to come here for comfort love
order me
let's be true

THE MAN WHO

(I)

Arrival

wasn't there again
today when they struck gold
on the Klondike wasn't there
when they opened up Oklahoma like a full belly
and the men ran in. some rode
horses, some rode down
men that stumbled on clubfoot and crutch, some on
foot leaped up under
the horses' throats to stick like burrs
scratch at the riders, scratch the horse out
from the earthrider, harry him in-
to the fat laid open from navel to breastbone the red
landgrab.

(II)

Nomination

i can name names
from rubbed coins, press heads
of old men, responsible
to speak for me
who in brass rage and in lead need of a just cause
or in gold
pain of a spent coin, ran in
to great Miklagard split open. they had bent
over the oars till salt glued them down. the skin
came off on the married wood. salt mats
in the hair stuck. salt glaze
on their cheeks hard-
ened to skin. their eyes,
salted down, lay in the barrels

of a red night that would not end. the wind
poured through their ears in vinegar gulf
streams. they were preserved
alive.
        Christ,   wasn't there
in Miklagard, the great keep beyond siege
when the oil bled when the steelmen
the ealdermen with a gold head on each cane stalk
with a stone ax in each hand striped
the great belly with a steel rail
grid when they broke
with the known tongues of their charted acres
their counted stones
and in an uncharted waste
made my blood

(III)

Campaign

at Dunkirk
the eyes drowned   i was not
with the dead or the living on the bloodtilled beach
they called Miklagard they called El
Dorado they called Ithica Utica Troy Rome Massena
Mycenae of the gold tombs, of the skin
and the hands and the eyes overlaid
with gold leaf to keep. they fell out
from the lost tongue and the used bones with a steel cap
in the kneecap with a steel plate
in the skull cup of the old friends
in the changed fields pressed close
to my glass skin to shout
even this shall be burnt off
                                        and ploughed up

the ground
                    sea
                          salt
                                    down belly for me and all
the finders the keepers
and the ship struck on the stone fields
and the rock crop and the heart's flag sang out
land   Warsaw   Auschwitz   Dachau
Belsen   Hiroshima   i will swear
by the red grid of my hot veins under glass
skin i was not there.
                                        let me lament
my grandfathers who turned
in the rich mint underground
harrow and rakehell plant
for my undoing. what was their good is
my evil. i can press heads
to serve.

(IV)

Election
of my sepulchre: they found
not all things new:
pleasure and pain do
still what they used to
and the name God, the plough
in the dark vault of the mouth, not
yet a word of art. my decent ones
my takers with a gold head
and the head gone in a just cause
with the heart cast out with the cause—when
in the salt waste of the green vines that stick
to my clean hands that eat

through my glass skin will the Friends send
in a tin box with a red cross a lament
for the decent ones for the makers
for the users for the breakers
of skin? nothing is changed.
i do their work, i am their wealth, i love the body
of their death. in the black box
with a steel plate where the bomb roots
with a hot snout i lament
the ramrod progress that splits me.
                                                            bear witness you
to the dead and the living in the belly of Selma Watts
with your small change in your clean hands
as the world turns in the shrill box
with the glass skin with the head gold
with the tongue gone with the eyes cut
down from their stalks in great Miklagard who but i
was massively absent my El
Dorado my city of man my belly
of death my promised plot
in the black box where the world ends
and on judgment day i
will not be there i
will not be.

BUZZARDS' BAY

it's a still backwater
it's a hard badwater
it's a damnyankee swamp each day
the owl and the pussycat put out
what the nextdoor owls have got
the owl is a pussy, the pussy's an owl
if she doesn't know when not
to if you marry me
i will scratch you a baby blue
out of each irish eye
comb from your hair with a steel fork
ten thousand clams to
chowder with you in the damp nights
when you limerick on down
to the fine sand and the mud black
with owl shells ripped off

don't say
what we both know is true
the love in me
will strip you

DR. POTATOHEAD TALKS TO MOTHERS

when you put on the feet be sure
the claws are attached long
three-toed when we landed
on the wetgreen planet in libra
the *three-toed* chef broke out
a gourmet spread frogs' legs
that had made the hop frozen
from baltimore / mushrooms
champagne /
when you put on
the hands that same day
the thumbs should not necessarily
oppose the dominant life forms
great big black buck mushrooms
undulated their velvet
blackribbed mouths flowed open
closed on us sucked our juices
and the monster frogs big as tanks
ripped off our navigator's
legs sautéed them in melted
rumpfat /
when you put on
the arms push in the pegs
deep so they can't be ripped
off in alpha centauri minced
frozen to fatten their giant
cats god we fought them
napalm and h-bomb blasted nine
planets and all the influences
out of the starry night
shivered
when you put on
the head when you put on

the head be very sure
the hat doesn't cover more
of them came when we landed we
landed half the universe
the hat should cover
the hair shelter the brain
from being baked powdered the ears
frozen we signed
treaties / what
to eat
but the eyes
uncovered

potatos we died
of boredom last week *but the eyes*
left open to spot what

we landed on x-37
in gemini giant potatos rolled
out riding fantastic tractors
of an unmeltable alloy
peeled off *but the eyes*
bare, freezing, spied out

our jackets
of skin dropped us flayed
and the teeth should be firmly planted
in hot water and boiled
yesterday when the dust
had settled we signed the treaty
we looked for something legal
to eat
and the teeth
there the mouth
open

PRIDE AT TEMPLE MOUNTAIN MINE

(I)

was built in
the stones they took out rang
the beautiful clean boast of men
like my grandpa kraus who came
gentle to brooklyntown
from having run guns in sinai / learned
the holy names of all
the minerals then known
to the brooklyn college of magic: "built
this town new and built it right."

see out of his stripped jawbones
rise up slag piled to the eyes
the seven deadly mines
wringing their hands
                                        to import-export-crash
when we all crashed some still
unborn as janitors to maintain
the premises of the chain
of movies owned by our brothers-in-law and it was
"a good job of carpentering"   /   they cry
                                                            not so long to wait now
                                                            when this bad time's dead
                                                            we'll come
                                                            into our own again

(II)

we can't put him down
the holy names
hel   azrael   siva   zeunerite

what's best in us a bright
green copper uranium arsenate
we ship out
to the indies now work
their passage back by night

not ignorant brutal goons
dropped the bomb made hell pay
gilt-edged and the ores chant
all deadly and very seven of them
to our highest power

if we could have our choice to be
what our dream was: Venial For A Day
you'd see how soon
(raze the Temple here / this
was what we came for) we'd
be Queen Of The May

AT MARY KATHLEEN, LUST

down under tell Mary Kathleen
i am doing very well here i lack
nothing the holes we work not
too dry not too damp but crowded
the workload . . .
                    to make a green plant
grow they brush each leaf
to keep off air from the West *under*
the mosquito net dirty thoughts
to keep a plant green / tell
Mary Kathleen *i thought last night to light*
the bloody niggers such a fire for God
they set the roots in semen
of men who eat no meat   such a complex
                                bisilicate of rare earths stuffed in-
                                to this hole to study . . .
to make the roots hold they strip
the soil of all rocks streaked
bright green or yellow they sell
these ores, taboo
                    yes
it goes well with me / is it still
well with you?
                  a treasury of practices
to dig out / *got up*
at seven   *under the netting*
let myself go carried a torch

for her steerage all the way
to white miners so many
brethren to set out here
pawing and dancing lost one
philadelphia dead these ten
years lost one
miami
to make a green man live till
harvest take the ores out
sell them then dance the sun out
the rain down lost
one down under one lost
screwing like mad *under the net* my dear
wife cries the livelong night and the light
lit / *the landscape lit in me*
voluptuous feelings under the rocks hide
till what fell out from the rain burns
bright yellow and green
up / tell Mary Kathleen
woke late / took
the census with a bearded
old man and i dead
these twenty years it is
Stillwellite with me

BLIND RIVER LOVE THAT MONEY SONG

one day last year i was walking along
that dingdong of an old year something B.C.
in British Columbia somebody took off
the whole top of the mountain to ya boys
whadaya say

well jesus what's a year sweet
red brown brannerite party-girl
what's two or three
when we could be on cloud
seventy-three glued in a matrix to
surround the time the deadhead walls fell down
easy together as ABC

why sweet potato tootsie will tell you james
bond madison in his grey
flannel pre-shrunk helmet find a way through
eighty miles of well
rounded quartz pebbles landed right off here
one day last year by somebody took off
1953 Blind River the most
kingsize trout deposit ever
to the nearest decimation
                    nellie
you can bet your bottom we'll be
happy you and i as dingdong B.C.
in scenic shoot-on-through

EAT 'EM UP SMITH TELLS ALL IN SOUTH AFRICA

when i lay back in my chair last night
the room was clean, the table white
as transvaal and the orange free state
were meant to be but when i came to
writhing verwoerts and up to dawn
cups and spoons had been thrown down
my head split where the yearsend riot
had just breezed through
                                        what you pass through
such places is nothing (as last night ran
down my throat shell of gold
aphroselma saffron of gold
and left me empty) but what remains
recovered as a by-
product after extracting the gold can do
with its wonder ingredient more for you
than aqua regia the devourer
monkshood wolfbane or black hellebore

sweetheart there never were more than four
in our grade A basic dirt
cheap rock bottom do-it-yourself sin kit
call them what you will. jack priest
laid down too many on that white cloth
to make his Numbers Al Chemical Trust
work out to a lucky seven
                                    pride
wrath   sloth   greed
for gold meat tail or just what
the other bastard's got
run through me wasted the whole night long
all splashed together / come daybreak
elixirs wise men have died

dreaming of / spiritus mundi
swells in me / gold
the aurum potabile, perfect
itself, can make no
perfection move in my bowels though
i swill it down like rain / water
hubris   /   anger
lethargy hunger can't make
that miracle drug work
my looped intestines straight
                                        i swear
i take no more in
than the body and blood of any man
i need to keep me new

the blacks are quiet, do no more
than what they're needed for
i swear i never eat
more than i have to have i swear
i never drink more
than belly and bowels can make room for
i swear the gold just shoots right through
like penicillin to leave a black
pitchblende lump i can't digest
and all the magic the priest charts
and einstein chants can't make stay in

some day i know i'll rest
content in my bed where pride
wrath   sloth   greed
will be in me always (strength rage

sleep need) stock
split or no split, yes, with a
halflife like that the action
will last one lifetime

WHAT MAISIE KNOW SHE DON'T WANT NO / ANGER GAME AT SHINKOLOBWE

well tonight the damnfool sunset pitched
a mustard-color homerun streak
right out over harlem heights / here i am
two thousand miles from katanga / see
how riots make all your high
flying love-ins ricochet how run-
away horses . . .
                                        here i am
curite so i can sleep late / hear
no mustard and orange rock wind up
the horses of the night / fly
them over the fence up the ramp / cut
down my two girls in hiroshima sack
nagasaki before it's time to rise and shine
breakfast all over the whole damn plate

well take it slow and easy friend
with the ornate bit look i'm no white
mercenary, want no big
game car, no hunt-club, arab-arms-race-horse run
to dream disasters
only to lie in bed latelazy
                                                        not
hear crazy katanga shoot off
in anger those great big jubilee balls
the fighting was all about patrice
dismumba and the big-pitch
opening all american game
in the a-bomb series dug
right up out of those prune-wrinkled black rocks

hey sweet
babe pretty mustard-sharp sun
of a fast gun two times out don't play
no anger game with this white child / don't shake
your shinkolobwe at me

HAPPY JACK'S ENVY

White Canyon chalky the gums
tooth stripped / brown spit
tobacco splat at your feet / a unique
minerology the ore
contains no vanadium is rich
in mixed sulphates: iron copper
i curse myself that ever
i came to this bleached place
and couldn't buy
the alternation
of sulphides that stinks
itself into sulphuric acid and copper
sulphate to attack
the primary ore pitchblende
that ever i came
to this bitch and couldn't
break down
to secondary uranyl sulphates / green
johannite green
uranopilate *yellow, quick, zippeite*
ere i die
came
to this thing here the first
time round a copper prospect sold
'46 one thousand smackeroos resold
'56 fifteen million / dear god came
to every cent of the body of this death
too late to live on it hope you rot in it yours
not mine and when i pray
in chalk dust kneel down / *give them*
on ground bones
the death they own

LETHARGY AT MI VIDA

Mi Vida   the weight
of this skin doesn't answer you
grey green the bones
push on through
broken the crust by a calcium
uranium
vanadate
tyuyamunite mi guel
i need the night
stopped up / you can see how black green
the way you need a bed
branch out
the way you need a friend
heavy the veins
not laces, nor any embracing here / coils
knot, tangle in Mi
Vida   corazon be very sure
it will
the sap thick sure
it will / it will not end

GEOMETRIES

nights i lie down to see you horribly dead
and throw the tears on the floor all night where they grow
under the press of my eyelids, smeared in a red
mash by the sinuous snake coils of my mind
crystals of blackdull coffinite, where they grow
and the children with you
a hydrated silicate of uranium which occurs
as a black impregnation in sandstone, where they roll
crazily glittering in corners under the bed
sprout, branch out, shifty in red-brown
renardite, torbernite with a green
crust fungus lacing its precious ore, with a green shine
like a lichen all over it, and they spring
jewel flowers of poison pastel out of the clean
fields in me.
if i see
under the press of my eyelids a death that has not
yet happened it is not now
nor can be history. if i see
the death that may not tomorrow or ever happen
under the press, that is not prophecy
as i have seen it smeared in the red
of my mind's true will.
and the children with you to throw
the tears on the floor where they grow
geometries of the will. oh i could lie down
with a new lover tomorrow
night i could walk all night
points sprouts shoots lines vines facets
surfaces that stick their planes one
to another, that stick sharp blocks
up out of moisture, air, their own salts
and not have to come home. sweetheart i could write

late sonnets not scanning the breakfast i must write
and the diapers must rhyme in the morning, my mind asleep
days
days wealth that is power to move out of space into space
geometries of the will nights
nights i could lie down to see you live, burst, roll
in crystals of black and green regret
polished, remembered, joy, every surface shine
crazily glittering in corners under the bed
and the children with you.
is it the way
salt bites into my tongue, is it the way
the antlers push up from the velvet skin
of the mind, sprout, crown and triumph the horned head
that will beat out on wood rock skin
the tattoo and the hot itch without will, that shakes, shivers,
will drum
matter on matter to break into heat? no matter:
the center that is my coherence will keep me whole,
as a black impregnation in sandstone, keep me cold
nights of crystal i sweat, tattoo and green
growth, fungus, cloud, force that moves force that is power to
move
and throw the tears on the floor
nights i lie down
to shiver you under the press of breakfast i must
skin (and it scans you too) in geometries
of the will fertile of tensions, shifty in red
brown renardite, where we grow where we grow
salts that are ground before tasted, crystals that show,
under the press that is not prophecy,
light stamped died beaten drummed into itself along sprouts
shoots, faults in the clean fields,

wealth that is power to move
space.
        sprout crown, triumph the tree on the head
where we spring in crystal and twig nets
geometries of the will, shape that we make
of ourselves, love that we make
our limit, coffinite we throw on the floor
all night
            triumph the horned head
where we grow.

SNOWMASS

my only jo and dearie o
in joyous gard i lay
with my bel ami all night
the pocked moon lit
my hair all year the pine cones let
drop thick fragrant oils on my head
on moss altars my hair was spread
wind eroded me sun
spiked in the daws' beaks picked at my eyes
three tall men rode astride
masks of the ashface gods down
the wind from snowmass peak
with a pointed stick dug
into my entrails straight through the navel balanced the staff
spun
rubbed to a spark and caught

my charged
blood shot up all day / all night
my teeth crackled blue sheet
thunder all that week
hard rock at my back and you dead
the nightmen roared in me the red chant
the white the greymask chant
from the east riding the air lit
the long fuse of my hair

NOTES

Persons:

Mike Fink	Mississippi river boatman, whose boast or "squeal" was "I'm half hoss, half alligator, and the meanest cuss alive."
Miguel de Unamuno y Jugo	name embedded in the ore, Tyuyamunite, in "lethargy at Mi Vida"

Places:

Happy Jack Mine	a uranium mine in Colorado
Blind River Mine	a uranium mine in Canada, the largest uranium deposit known
Temple Mountain Mine	
Shinkolobwe Mine	a uranium mine in Katanga. ore from the Congo was used to make the first A-bombs.
Mary Kathleen Mine	a uranium mine in Australia
Mi Vida Mine	

Ores:

Pitchblende	Stillwellite
Uranite	Brannerite
Zeunerite	Curite

Johannite
Uranopilate
Zippeite
Tyuyamunite
Coffinite
Renardite
Torbernite

PS3569 H44 U7 1969
+Uranium poems. +Sherwin, Judith
0 00 02 0210590 4
MIDDLEBURY COLLEGE